The Shits that made me an Overthinker

CRESTY XAVIER

to my moon

I thank God with all my heart for the grace, strength, and quiet inspiration that carried me through the creation of this book. There were moments of stillness, doubt, and wonder along the way, but through it all, I felt a guiding presence—gentle yet unwavering. This work is not just a collection of words, but a reflection of something deeper that I could not have shaped on my own. For the clarity of thought, the flow of ideas, and the courage to see it through, I give thanks to the one who makes all things possible.

For the dreamers

This book is a collection of 200 thought-provoking and meditative writings, each created with the intention of inspiring moments of deep reflection and introspection. When I set out to write this, my hope was to offer you a space for personal exploration and growth, where you could connect with the words in a way that feels natural and meaningful to you.

Rather than reading it cover to cover in a traditional sense, I invite you to approach it differently. Randomly select a page and allow the writing you find there to be your guide for that moment. Read it carefully, let it settle into your mind, and give yourself the space to reflect on its meaning. The blank space left on each page is yours to fill—whether with your thoughts, emotions, questions, or insights that arise as you engage with the words.

In this way, each page becomes a personal conversation between you and the writing, a quiet exchange of ideas that invites you to slow down, listen to your inner voice, and discover what resonates with you at that particular moment. The reflections you write are not just about the text itself, but about you-your own thoughts, beliefs, and feelings as you navigate the pages.

I encourage you to approach this book not with the pressure to 'finish' it, but with the intention of savouring the process of reflection, allowing each piece of writing to serve as a stepping stone toward greater mindfulness and understanding. My hope is that through this practice, you will find moments of clarity, growth, and connection, both with the words on the page and with yourself.

Cresty Xavier

April 2025

felix lectio'

You are a shooting star
with the ability to glow by your own.

Your destiny is to travel
from one end of the cosmos to the other,
exploring the mysteries
and illuminating others.

But you are often drawn in
by the so-called gravity of the planets
that only shines with your light.

You overthink things-
and connect the erroneous dots
that are only apparent to you,

Simply disregarding the ones
that leads you to the truth
and killing the happiness within you.

Believe me mate,
Your life is exactly like-
The best lyrics of your favourite song.

Create a path of your own
If you are confused about choosing between-

The 'one less traveled' and
The 'one more traveled'.

It's okay to feel fine
if your best friend doesn't understand you,

Because it took over a million years
for mankind to realize
that the world was not flat,
but round.

It's okay to practice sitting alone,
because in the end,
you'll be alone in your tomb.

They may label you as weird,
for they find it hard to see that,

The brilliance you carry-
is pure genius, wild and free.

Dear mate,
all you need
is a hug to feel better.

I reiterate —
a genuine hug.

If you want to cry, cry.
If you want to laugh, laugh.
If you want to hate, hate.

Be like clouds —
simple,
and weightless.

Being a river is so complicated,
Forced to cleanse itself,

Yet purify others.

Dear mate,
You hold the greatest gift of all —
The ability to love.

Love is so powerful,
It can even sway
The goddess of mischief.

Maybe it's because you only see
The darkest part of yourself,
A villain in your own eyes.

But believe me, mate,
You are greater than that.

Even though you work hard,
and feel unsatisfied with what you've done,
it's a sign —
you are destined
to create your own legacy.

Overthinking is a helper —
It fills the gaps,
It connects the dots,
And, of course,
It helps you
Kill yourself faster.

Being a soldier
Who saves his opponent
Is far greater
Than an emperor
Who murders monarchs.

Don't believe in trailers,
some may have the best trailers
but a worst end.

But some others
may not even have a trailer
but ends up being best.

Maybe all you need
is some haters in your life,
to understand your worth.

Life hits hard
when you realize-
that even music
can't heal you.

Maybe all you need
is a pen,
paper,
and a coffee —
to write your future.

Bro,
it's your trust she needs the most,
not your promises.

You are not built
to always choose right.

Mistakes will happen, brothers —
they're a part of your life.

It's okay
if you're not the most powerful person in the room.

But you play an important role
in making the room powerful.

You are unique.

You are hard to define,
hard to explain.

You are mysterious —
and that's better,
because no one can manipulate you.

24

Don't wait for the right time,
There is no such time as called 'right time'.
It's all in your head,
It's all about your mentality.

If you find your perfect love,
With all due respect,
Please don't lose her,
My friend.

It was not your fault
That you misunderstood
Your best friend.

You both were perfect friends
That even Philotas
Was jealous of you.

Your friendship was so perfect
That it even angered the gods.
Your friendship was a curse for them.

There is plenty of love out there in the world.
Don't lose hope in searching
for the best one meant for you.
Yours is only one hug away.

Maybe we are all standing
Before the right door,
But with the wrong key.

Memories are something
You should control —
Don't let them
Take control over you.

You deal with a lot of problems at once,
that's why you're not getting
a proper solution for all of it.

Prioritize your problems,
deal with them systematically —
solutions will follow you.

Maybe you are far from the answer,
But still, it's better
Than not having an answer.

32

All you need is a chair near a window.

Hug your mom —
she deserves it
more than your partner.

Like the key,
you should turn yourself
towards the right direction
to open your fortune.

You get the best variant
when you blend the right colors.
Likewise, find the best color
to create the best version of you.

It's better to be
a half-filled bottle
with pure water
than a whole bottle
with tainted water.

Save your memories in your heart,
as you save starred messages on WhatsApp.
Trash your past,
like you delete your ex's WhatsApp account.

Give priorities to those who love you,
as you pin the contacts you love
to chat the most.

It's okay to find red light in your life,
it's a sign that you need to re-energize
in order to move on more quickly.

The power you earn
comes from the anguish you experience.

Feel okay to
Hug your father,
Kiss your mom,
Greet your brother.

It means a lot to them—
Just do it, mate!

42

You are gorgeous
as you are,
in front of your favorite mirror.

As you clip your clothes to the rope
from falling down,
clip yourself with your favorite tribe
from losing yourself.

Maybe the devil overthink much
that he cannot be an angel again.

When you're unsure about saying yes,
There is no middle ground.

Dear mate,
don't be sad for what you gave in the past,
it's all coming back twice as fast.

The love you expressed,
the trust you gave,
the faith you showed—
everything.

Better to hunt the past
than be hunted by it.

Cristiano and Marcelo
Ragnar and Athelstan
Thor and Loki
Harry and Hermione
You and Me—
Bliss!

Don't let your 3am thoughts to fade away,
they're the messages delivered by your soul.

Love her as if it's your last day with her.
Respect her as she is your queen.
Protect her as she is your sole status.

Maybe you are like an albatross,
the wicked may reject you,
but still, you are forced
to show the signs to the nobles.

You deserve to be loved back
the way you once loved your first love.
The love that was so pure,
the love that was so innocent.

Capture all the happy moments,
'cause that's all we have in the end.

54

Being bold in your crisis
is like sharpening your attitude,
just as you sharpen a pencil.

The so-called silly things you do for love
are the ones that make your love
worth even more.

Them:
"perfect society doesn't exist."

Me:
"metaverse."

Sometimes, we should prefer
taking the U-turn in our life,
in order to see
the way we came through.

58

I'm a person who prefers
parallel roads rather than main roads.

She is a beautiful red rose,
her beauty lies underneath her sharpened thorns.

I like the part of me,
who dances in an empty room,
putting my earphones in
and playing my favourite song.

The better version of you
is still greater than what you possess.
Work hard,
grab it, brother.

She is bold,
her boldness lies
between her tears.

She is like an eagle,
with the power to rise
above the clouds,
above the mountains.

But she is bound,
trapped within the cages
of her own tears.

It's better to be like a black hole,
so no one knows what's inside of you—
you will remain mysterious.

They say music heals,
but have you ever felt a pain so deep
that even music couldn't mend?
Life hits different then.

She is the west wind
that brings peace and calmness.

Happiness is her soulmate,
in her, we find pleasure.

Yet, we often fail
to give her value.

She loves the beautiful sunset,
wishing she could be the sun.
But she often forgets
the fire within its core.

She loves the fragrance of freedom,
drifting in a lonely ship,
amid the ocean—
undivided by boundaries,
untouched by nations.

There are days
when she wishes to be the wind.

On other days,
she longs to be the clouds,
to be everywhere,
spreading love and peace.

But the vicious walls
always block her path.

Being a bird,
she dreams of traveling north,
all the way from the south.

Singing her favourite songs,
refreshing and relieving everyone's pain,
without knowing
she doesn't have much life left.

Being emotionally stable
doesn't mean you must
always control your feelings.

Maybe it's okay
to express them wholeheartedly
sometimes.

It's better to remember your old playlist,
it may act like a bridge
to your good old days.

Maybe your good old days aren't over yet,
now is just an interval
for the best days to come.

She doesn't want to be
the princess of the realm.

She prefers to be
the queen of her own identity.

If you find your
divine soulmate,

With all respect, my dear friend,
please don't let her slip away—
not for the *so-called* things in your life.

Sitting together with him,
she was creating her realm,
letting her king know
the boundaries of their new kingdom,
naming their beautiful palace—Camelot.

It's alright
that you don't always understand everything.

Maybe the right one will come into your life,
and make you capable
of understanding even better.

It's okay to remove people from your life,
like tearing pages from your favourite book.

It hurts both ways,
but maybe, it's worth doing.

Being the king and emperor of our own minds,
we are all destined
to build our own Camelot.

Maybe the song
you normally skip from your playlist
will be the one to lift your spirit
when you're feeling low—
when all your favourite songs fail to do so.

We are not destined by external forces,
we are destined by our own potential.

82

Life hits differently
when we realize
that even sleep
isn't enough
to overcome our tension.

You are stressed out,
called your favourite number,
shared your pains,
got relieved,
felt relaxed again—
bliss...!!

Don't let those numbers
slip away from your life.

84

At some point in life,
having and creating a vision
is more complicated
than working for it.

If life gives you a chance
to be the best soulmates,
be like Messi and Antonella.

It was the first wave of COVID-19,
locking ourselves in our homes,
spending time watching series,
playing games—
life was good.

Now, it's the nth wave of COVID-19—
vice-versa.

It's so blissful
to have someone who calls you
when you're sick,
waiting for your recovery.

Sometimes,
it's more than blissful.

Through the windows,
she sees her future—
so close, yet out of reach.

But she is bound within that room,
her tears forming chains,
holding her back from stepping outside.

Be compassionate,
be caring,
be loving.

Be a northern light
in someone's life.

Choosing money over love,
choosing love over money—
these are two extremes.
Choose your extreme wisely.

Sometimes you want to be
the tiniest creature in the universe,
to observe everything in its entirety.

92

Don't give up your love on her,
she has seen the worst side of love,
the only thing she needs is time
to understand your true love.

Sometimes you choose to be in sadness,
in order to know how much worth the pain was,
and it's okay to be so.

Give solutions,
not advice.

It's okay to be on the
wrong path,
but make sure that
your direction is right.

96

Satisfying others' souls,
you often forget to
satisfy your soul,
and that's the greatest
mistake in your life.

You send a message to her,
she replied mocking back.
You overthink it,
wishing you never sent that message—
lol.!

Being the fallen angel
doesn't mean that she is the evil one.
Maybe she was betrayed
by the so-called devils in heaven.

You just realized that,
today, you had an unproductive day?
Nah, bro, today you just
reflected on your life.
That's it...

Life is like adjusting the notes
with the right instrument in your hand.

Everyone will reach a point
in their lives
where a single decision,
made in that moment,
will determine
the rest of their lives.

Some may even have
the ability to manipulate
the evil spirit—
by pretending
they are mentally weak.

You see the real
beauty of your soul
when you cry.

Some people have
an influence in your life
so strong,
they can even change
your favourite playlist.

Maybe all you need
is some time-
to change.

Of course,
you can recreate your past—
by rectifying your mistakes.

There are two kinds of people:
the ones who manifest
others' legacy,
and the ones
who manifest
their own.

We all have transformed—
from enjoying the game
in front of the computer,
to play the same game
just to escape reality.

The best part of the show
is when we unknowingly transform—
from hating the villain
to loving him.

110

Yes, you fell from the sky,
but that doesn't mean
you don't have the option
to rise up there again.

Lack of conviction
is the greatest barrier
you'll ever face
on the path to success.

Divide and rule
was the greatest strategy
used by emperors
to conquer other nations.

Perhaps, not only emperors—
but even gods
have practiced it.

Maybe the portal
to your own destruction
is opened
by the fear within you.

114

There will be a situation
where the hero in you
is saved
by the underrated villain
within you.

Today or tomorrow,
we all tend to make
a promise to someone
at some point in time—
and our life
depends on it.

116

It's fine to change your priorities
as you get older,
but make sure
they remain focused
on you.

Perhaps it's okay
to sacrifice our greatest pleasure
for the sake
of future grandeur.

If you want to make your
name known to the world,
compete with the names
that the world already knows.

Design an epic move
which shapes your destiny.

Pain is what shapes your future,
suffering is what sharpens it.

She is like the wind,
nobody knows her path.
She flows with a scent,
undisturbed by the chaos,
she wanders.

122

She smells enchanting,
she showers blessings.
No one can hate her,
she redefines happiness.

She is guided by her own rules,
with her own values,
with her own ethics.
She is busy building her realm.

Best friend, stabbed through the heart-
by an ambitious man.
Brother, murdered by a purple man.
Sister, killed out of her own greed.
Father, killed out of his own love.

Being god is hard,
playing god is harder.

Rage and vengeance.
Anger and pain.
Loss and regret.

The greatest weapon
that shapes a man.

The toughest battle
a man should pursue alone.

Night is calm,
night is beautiful,
night is gorgeous.

But no one wishes
that it could stay forever.

The journey of that breeze,
the cold breeze of 3 a.m.
Refreshing others,
enlightening others,
spreading calm,
spreading love.

Be that cold breeze
in others' lives.

As an overthinker,

I prefer reading books
rather than watching films,
so that
I can create my own
Camelot in my gorgeous city.

A little bit of jealousy
makes a relationship far better,
maybe more interesting.

I repeat—
a little bit of it.

Immortality becomes a curse
when you start understanding
the point that
you have no life left.

The sign spells—
into the future,
into the past.

I prefer going back
to my past
with all the knowledge
i've acquired,
so i will not
be cheated again.

132

You should knowingly
let people go from your life.
You should knowingly
avoid celebrating
weekend parties.

It's like sharpening the pencil
to get an acute edge.

You should get rid of
the negative individual in your life,
in order to have a clearer view
of the future—

Much as you would
get rid of the curtains
to appreciate
the nicer surroundings.

Did you ever have a feeling
that someone is standing
next to you...?

It's not a ghost.
It's your other entity—
your fully potential entity—
standing over there,
blaming you
because you are not
able to attain it.

Design a prosperous future plan,
like you create
your favourite Spotify playlist.

136

You all have your own
visions,
don't let
ordinary people
reshape
your extraordinary visions.

Choose love,
not lust.

138

When you notice something is popular,
it doesn't mean it is
the perfect one that exists.

We all have our own
3 a.m. Playlist
that we don't want
others to know.
It's highly classified,
it's purely bonded with our soul.

Overthinking is like
a venom,
which eats and rests within you.
It's a parasite.

Dear best friend,
it's okay that you don't feel
the same way about me as
you did before.
It's alright and quite natural.
We can't always love the same song forever.
Our priorities will change,
our taste will change.
It's not your fault.

142

Our trust issues are so toxic
that sometimes we
don't even trust our own laptop
camera in zoom/teams meetings.

THE SHITS THAT MADE ME AN OVERTHINKER

There are some situations in which
we often get our favourite things,
but we leave them untouched.
We don't care at all,
but we are satisfied just owning them.

Guess what—
red flag or not?

144

If we get whatever
we wish easily in our life,
then you're operating
the pirated version
of your life.

We hate toxicity,
but we often bury
the truth that it
is the base on which
mankind is built.

146

Somewhere between
the two alternatives
lies your true life.

It's okay to create fake scenery in our
head for our satisfaction.
Maybe it's okay to find happiness in it.

If you have seen the bottom,
you are worth enough to experience
its other polar.

Everyone finds happiness
when she blossoms earlier.
But no one notices
that she will be the first to perish.

Being the fastest, heaviest, and
strongest in the group,
he considered himself a hyena.
But he often forgets the
presence of the wolf in the scene.

The dark part of our life,
the hidden part,
the most hated part—
the part where we all encountered a zombie.

A zombie that stays with us
throughout our lives,
a zombie we wish we didn't have.

But we often forget
that is the same reason
we lead a life where we are still alive—
a life where we are not dead.

It's okay to have a dead part in our life—
a part we wish we didn't have.
But remember, that part-
is the motivator to lead a better life.

We love the sunset,
wishing that it could last a little longer.
We love the night,
wishing that it had the best moon.
But we often fail to applaud
the same sun at noon,
which shines brighter,
and the same moon at night,
which shines less.

Maybe you are not abandoned—
you are watched from a distance,
as in the case of the exodus,
to find the real importance
of being you.

154

Lights are good,
but not all lights
serve the same purpose.

A beautiful sculpture,
made with the finest metal.
Men had eyes on its imperfections.

Touched by an ambitious man—
he laid his hands on it.
The sculpture lost its beauty,
thrown away to the darkness.

But still, it exemplifies its beauty—
not outside,
indeed, inside.

Life is like a cave,
untouched by man,
protected by nature.

Deep inside, it hides
a valuable treasure
held throughout the ages.

Man tries to explore it,
but the dark soldier rests deeper.
Beheld by fear,
no one ever enters the cave.

Trust is like the garden of Eden
once lost,
it's lost forever.

Sometimes you need to
concentrate more on the borders
of your painting—
how you specifically and carefully
finish the border.

Maybe a single mistaken
outline
can destroy the whole painting.

It doesn't matter how big
the scripture on our tombstone is,
if you didn't have a heart
as big as the tomb exemplifies.

Eden—
the most beautiful
mankind had ever seen.
Blessed to have it,
but cursed by the greed
of an ambitious man,
mankind lost it.

Out of fear,
the Eden Garden disguised itself,
not having the strength
to bear another curse.

We often come across this Eden Garden,
but we fail to notice it.

The Eden believes that one day,
the perfect one will find it.
And Eden will stay with them
forever.

Forget the moon,
give preference
to the little stars
that shines by their own light
in the dark sky.

You look up to the sky, you see
that little star shining bright
in the night sky.

But have you ever wondered—
when did that star
produce the light we see now?

Maybe it took
millions of light years
to reach our eyes.

Maybe, within that time,
the star
had already perished.

But still,
we don't notice the effort
that the star took,
and we don't think
of that star.

You wear your favourite dress,
you look excited,
you look gorgeous—
you had the day.

You don't value
the opinion of others.
It's all up to you.

Your dress,
your happiness.
That's it.

Your dress also plays
a part
in your happiness.

They are still watching you,
counting upon
the fault in your stars.

Drive yourself
to the safe zone,
where others may not find you.

They will
eventually
fed up counting you.

In the worst,
you may find
the gem
you're looking for.

Isn't it so wonderful
to know
that some painful scratches
bring the most
beautiful sketches?

In the heights of fame,
glorified by others
in the hall of fame,

Everyone often forgets
the depth of the fall—
unless he slips
from the height.

Mind is like the night sky.
In order to get a clearer view,
there should not be
any dark clouds.

Likewise, to understand
and control your mind,
you don't need others' opinions—
yourself is far more necessary.

It's okay that you change for others,
but be aware
that you don't change
your desired destiny
for that.

A pencil too pointed may break
at any point of time,
turning it useless.
Perfection doesn't always
link with appearance—
it's always linked
with the usefulness of it.

Overtaking can be related
with the different phases of life.

In both cases,
we need confidence—
that you have enough willpower
to change the gear
and upgrade.

172

We may do have
several lives,
we're born different
in all lives.

I think,
they were fated
to be together
in this life.

She stretched her branches
across his trunk,
he expanded his leaves
across her body.

They were born different,
but built together.

Their love can't be divided—
even by a different life.

There will be several
unexpected curves
in our lives.

It's part of the journey,
in order to make
our life
more beautiful.

We all are bonded
to some specific areas
in which our heart
is stuck with.

Don't let it
slip away from you—
you are unique
in your own weirdness.

Getting the desired photos
makes us happy.

The tree lost
its beautiful leaves.

The fallen ones—
they were depressed enough to find
that they have no purpose anymore.

They were depressed
of losing their part
in the beauty of the tree.

But they often fail to recognize
that they were fallen
in a position
that creates more beautiful scenery.

How can the great tree
let its beautiful leaves fall away
without valuing them?

Maybe the wrong road
let you get
more experience.

You are the northern light,
no one can ever imagine
the beauty of you—
unless they experience it.

You forget to focus
on the things
which are more clear
to you —

And you often try
to focus
on the things
which are far away,
and
cannot be focused.

You can't satisfy
your soul
and your body
at the same time.
If you're doing it—
you're not human.
You're playing god.

Not admired by anyone,
isolated from everyone,
he was satisfied
with his own creation.

Being god,
he named it,
supervised it—

Never letting
anyone know,
never revealing
that, for him,
they all worked.

It was a curse
to her—
having the best scent
in the room.

Often,
she was forced to produce it
all day
for the sake of others.

She was manipulated.

But it all
shaped her
to produce
the better version
of herself.

Dear friend,

Among the red roses,
you are the only one in white.

The red rose's thorns
have the potential
to crush you.

However,
you frequently forget—
you are the only one
in your class
capable of living longer
than the red rose,
which will perish
within a short
period of time.

Not being
the smartest
in the group,

Not being
the bravest
in the group,

Not being
the topmost
in the group—
He was still
happy
with what he had.
After all,

Humans
created
hierarchy.

Maybe
he was sent
from above.

Perhaps
he is
above
the fray.

You're that one chocolate
I often keep
hidden from others.

Sitting quietly
in the corner of my room,

Savouring the moments,
giving the worthiness
it deserves.

Speeding up—
the ones who go down
were often noticed
by those who climbed
the steps.

They were praised
for their speed.

But they were ignorant
of the fact:

The speed they gained
was born
from their own
descent.

Guarded
by mighty statues
and enormous gates,
She cast her fear
out of sight.
She protected
her realm—
blissfully.

You should focus
on building
your own Atlantis—
rather than coaching
others.

Because if not—
when the sea
swallows Atlantis,

You
will be
the only one
they hold
responsible.

Her hug—
so toxic,

It wasn't easy,
even for the sane,
to see
it was fake.

Friend,
you are about
to reach your Avalon.

The distance—
not so far.
The only thing is:

Don't quit
so fast.

As the quote says,
"great things take time."

We see the wrong
in others—

But often,
we fail to notice
we are bound
by the same mistakes.

192

In his grief,
he fails to notice—

His mood
destroys
his company too.

We are all bonded
with the power of magic
within us—

But we often
don't pronounce
the right spell.

194

Nothing hurts more
than losing
your favorite keychain—

The one you've cherished
above all the universe.

The right person will come
into your life—

Helping you lift the Excalibur
that you can't lift
by yourself.

Bonded by fear,
he was too afraid to express his love.
Fear of losing her,
he always hid his love
deep within his heart,
not letting anyone find it.

She wears a mask
to disguise herself,
believing the right one
will find her.

And when he does,
seeing her true beauty,
he will stay forever.

198

Being the cast one,
he had known life
in its fullest.
He tasted both the best
and the worst
of it.

The sky sheds her tears,
wiping away the weight of past mistakes.
Ready to love again,
she fills herself with love,
conspiring with the stars
for the arrival of her moon.

The rain always brings me happiness—
the cold breeze,
the good smell,
everything.

Rain symbolizes something
our mind quietly longs for—
the things we wish
we never let slip
from our lives.

About the author

Cresty Xavier is a social worker and counsellor based in UAE, with a background in medical and psychiatric social work. With a deep passion for mental health and emotional well-being, he has worked extensively in schools and educational institutions, guiding individuals through personal and psychological challenges.

Holding a master's degree in social work with a specialization in medical and psychiatry, Cresty has gained experience in counselling, crisis intervention, and career guidance. His journey includes working with individuals facing mental health struggles, conducting rehabilitation programs, and assisting in therapeutic interventions.

Driven by the belief that self-awareness and emotional resilience are key to personal growth, he continues to explore new ways to support and uplift those in need. With a commitment to lifelong learning, he remains dedicated to expanding his knowledge and making a meaningful impact in the lives of others.

www.ingramcontent.com/pod-product-compliance
Lightning Source LLC
Chambersburg PA
CBHW061339160726
47995CB00001B/90